CHINA

by
Gail B. Stewart

CRESTWOOD HOUSE
New York

Collier Macmillan Canada
Toronto

Maxwell Macmillan International Publishing Group
New York   Oxford   Singapore   Sydney

Library of Congress Cataloging-in-Publication Data
Stewart, Gail, 1949-
    China / by Gail B. Stewart. — 1st ed.
        p.   cm.—(Places in the news)
    Summary: Examines historic and recent events that have kept China in the news.
    ISBN 0-89686-538-X
    1. China—Politics and government—1949- —Juvenile literature. [1. China—History—1949-]
I. Title. II. Series: Stewart, Gail, 1949-   Places in the news.
DS777.75.S77   1990
951.05—dc20   90-35497
                                                                                              CIP
                                                                                               AC

Photo Credits
Cover: Magnum Photos, Inc.: (Stuart Franklin)
Magnum Photos, Inc.: (Stuart Franklin) 4, 39; (Bruno Barbey) 10, 16, 20; (Rene Burri) 26;
    (P. Jones Griffiths) 29; (Abbas) 32
AP—Wide World Photos: 13, 23, 35, 43

CRESTWOOD HOUSE

Macmillan Publishing Company   Collier Macmillan Canada, Inc.
866 Third Avenue   1200 Eglinton Avenue East
New York, NY 10022   Suite 200
                                                        Don Mills, Ontario M3C 3N1

Produced by Flying Fish Studio Incorporated

Printed in the United States of America

First Edition

10 9 8 7 6 5 4 3 2 1

CONTENTS

In the spring of 1989, thousands of Chinese students gathered in Tiananmen Square seeking democratic reforms. Their peaceful protest turned violent when soldiers were ordered to attack and kill them.

CHINA IN THE NEWS

In June 1989 a tragedy occurred in China. Thousands of people were killed, and many thousands more were injured. It was not a battle, but a massacre.

The victims were young Chinese men and women, many of them university students. They were killed by the Chinese army, under the direction of the most powerful man in China, Deng Xiaoping.

Newspapers around the world called the incident "the blood-bath in Beijing," for it occurred in that capital city. Most Chinese who witnessed the massacre were in tears. They saw friends shot down, crushed by huge army tanks, and stabbed by bayonets. One student waved his friend's shirt—soaked in blood—as a flag. "We shall not forget this," sobbed the youth.

The students had gathered in a large open area called Tiananmen Square. They had come seven weeks earlier to protest laws they felt were unfair. The demonstration began with a few thousand people; then the numbers climbed. By the time of the massacre, the crowd had grown to more than one million people.

Their goal was to protest in a nonviolent, peaceful way. They were unarmed. They sang songs of unity and protest. They made speeches. They linked arms and chanted. But many of them were unprepared for the violent attack that the government ordered.

One witness recalled trucks filled with troops smashing through student barricades. As the trucks sped through the square, they knocked down hundreds of students. Hundreds more were shot as

5

the soldiers in the trucks sprayed bullets everywhere.

Seventy or eighty students tried to turn back a tank. Waving and smiling at the soldiers inside, they sat in front of an unmoving tank. "We were trying to convince the soldiers to join us," remembers one of the group. "We called out to them to come join us in our quest for democracy and goodwill."

The soldiers ignored the friendly waves of the students. They chose, instead, to drive the vehicle straight ahead. Too late, the students realized their protest had turned into a mass suicide. Most were crushed to death beneath the heavy tank.

Peaceful protests happen quite often in the United States and other countries. Some of these protests are by workers desiring higher wages. Others involve people who feel that they are being treated unfairly or who want laws changed. No one at these protests ever expects them to result in death or injury, although they sometimes do.

People had hoped that the student protests in China would not end in violence, either. In fact, since they had gone on for almost two months without bloodshed, the protests were at first considered a success. Up until the army attack, the students thought that they had made a point—that many people were not satisfied with the way the Chinese government was being run.

The events leading to the army attack at Tiananmen Square thrust China into the headlines around the world. Everyone read about the problems between Chinese government officials and the people. Most were astonished at the news of the attack. Even the reporters and diplomats who spend much of their time learning about China were shocked.

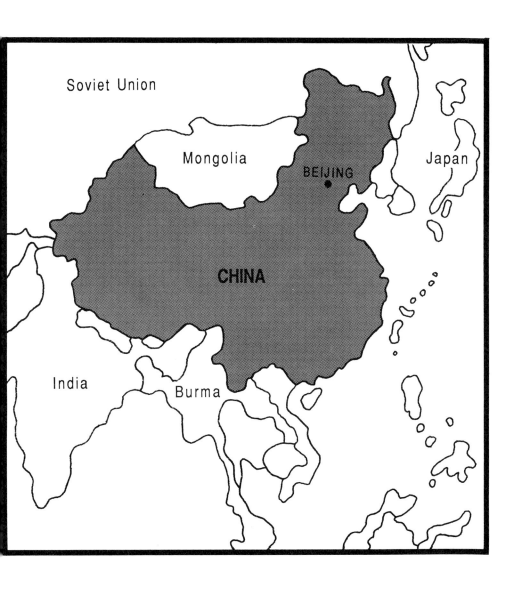

The events did not end in Tiananmen Square. They continue today and are being felt not just in China but around the world. Nations that trade with China are especially concerned. Is the country changing? they wonder. Are there deep problems in China that cannot be resolved? Some of China's trading partners, including the United States, wonder if China is heading toward civil war.

It is difficult for some to understand how this tragic massacre could have happened. A look at the events that led up to it, however, can help explain why thousands of students went to Tiananmen Square and why they died there.

However shocking the massacre was to experts, they all seem to agree on one thing: Deng Xiaoping was in trouble in his homeland. Although he had won the battle with the students, he had lost the trust and faith of many of the Chinese people. In November 1989, the 85-year-old leader turned over military power in China to his handpicked successor, Jiang Zemin.

Some historians have noted that Deng acted much like another powerful Chinese leader, Mao Tse-tung. Mao was the most influential leader in China in this century. So it is also helpful to learn something about Mao and the history of China before the massacre to understand Deng's orders to the soldiers at Tiananmen Square.

MODERN CHINA IS BORN

China is a vast land. More than one billion people live within its borders. More people live in China than anywhere else on earth. Many of them live in the large cities in the eastern half of the country. However, most Chinese are farmers who inhabit the rural areas of the nation.

China is one of the oldest civilizations in the world. For thousands of years, the country was ruled by a series of powerful kings. Because most Chinese were poor, uneducated farmers—peasants, they were called—it was not difficult for an emperor and his armies to take control. For dozens of centuries before Deng Xiaoping was born, China was governed by kings who had little respect for the peasants.

The Coming of Mao

Modern China really began in 1949. It was then, just after World War II, that China's leadership and government changed dramatically.

A young man named Mao Tse-tung, along with a large group of his followers, seized the government. They believed in communism. Communism is a way of organizing a society. Communists

believe that no group should be above any other group. All should be treated equally. No individual or family should have more wealth or property than any other. And no individual or family should be more powerful than any other. The power in a communist society should lie with all the people. The state, not individuals, should own all businesses and land. These are the things Mao and his fellow Communists believed.

A Country in Despair

The China that Mao took over in 1949 was in need of great changes. The power lay not with the people but with rich landlords. They owned large plots of land and used peasants as slaves to farm the land.

Medical care was very poor; what existed was available only for the wealthy. The vast majority of Chinese—more than 80 percent—could neither read nor write. Even though writing existed in China from ancient times, only the scholars and upper classes actually knew how to do it.

In addition to these problems, many of the customs common among the peasants were based on old-fashioned thinking. For instance, many families were angry when a girl baby was born. They thought girls were of no use, since they simply married and moved away. Another female in the family meant only another mouth to feed, without getting much in return.

In those days, no one thought women or girls could do important work on farms. They were considered valuable only for cooking and caring for young children. Because women were valued so little, it was common practice before the days of Mao for families to drown or abandon female babies.

Another ancient custom was foot-binding. Because girls and young women were thought of as unimportant, they were often treated as dolls or toys. Families did not consider their daughters' health or comfort. They were mainly concerned with making the girls as attractive as possible so they could find husbands. When a girl was very young, her family wound long strips of cloth tightly around her feet. The cloth prevented the girl's feet from growing properly. Her feet stayed tiny and deformed and much too small to support her body. Because of this, she walked with tiny, quick steps, which were considered dainty and beautiful.

These customs and other dangerous practices were outlawed by Mao in 1949. He felt that women were as important as men. Killing female babies and binding feet became criminal acts under Mao's rule. So, too, was selling one's children as slaves. Mao believed that all human life had dignity and worth. The peasants were, after all, the people. And under the form of government called communism, the people ruled.

Revolution Is a Painful Process

Mao made many changes in China. He called it a revolution, because the whole style of life had to change. But, he warned the people, revolution was not easy. It could not happen overnight. It was a process—and a painful one, at that.

In 1949 Mao Tse-tung and his Communist followers gained control of China. Over the next 27 years, he revolutionized Chinese life.

Besides his reforms in the treatment of women, education, and health care, Mao changed the farming system. He forced rich landlords to give up their land and turn it over to the peasants. Millions of people were killed during this revolution. Those wealthy and powerful landlords accused by the government of unfairly treating the peasants were executed. In fact, anyone who opposed Mao and his revolution was killed.

Mao kept reminding people that this violence was necessary to change their country. It was part of the painful process he had warned them about. If China was, indeed, to become a classless society, where all people were truly equal, the peasants had to break out of their chains. There was no room for rich landlords or greedy businessmen.

Tightening Controls on the People

China was not the only nation governed by Communists. The Soviet Union had gone through a similar revolution in 1917. China looked to the Soviet Union for advice on how to make communism work.

However, even with Soviet guidance, Mao was not satisfied. He did not think China was moving forward as quickly as he had hoped it would. Part of the problem was the difficulty of feeding China's large population. The farmers were having trouble growing enough food for all the people.

To solve the problem, Mao decided to take the land back from the peasants. For efficiency, he divided the land into larger sections and had many families work these large new farms together. Anywhere from 15 to 30 families lived on these "collective farms," as they were called.

As years went by, however, Mao still was unsatisfied. The peasants did not seem to be interested in farming land they did not own themselves. Planting and harvesting went slowly. Often the farmers neglected the crops completely.

In response, Mao put the farms under the control of the state. Peasants were paid to work on the farms, just as laborers were paid to work in the factories. Fewer and fewer freedoms existed under Mao's rule. The government made almost all the decisions. What to plant, where to plant, and when to harvest were decisions farmers had no control over.

"Let One Hundred Flowers Bloom"

In 1956 Mao gave a speech in which he ordered, "Let one hundred flowers bloom together; let one hundred ideas contend." He thought that communism was working quite well in China. He felt secure enough about his success that he would allow people to criticize the government. In the United States, we call this "freedom of expression"—the right to speak what is on our minds. Sometimes our thoughts are critical; sometimes they are complimentary. Either way, we are allowed by our Constitution to express ourselves freely.

Mao's "hundred flowers" idea seemed popular with many people. The country's most educated people, the intellectuals,

During the Cultural Revolution, Mao relied on the patriotism of China's young people to carry out his ideas against freedom of thought. He organized them into a military-like group called the Red Guard.

16

began to speak out about the communist system. However, their opinions were not pleasing to Mao's ears! Most of the intellectuals expressed critical views. They complained that China's people were not allowed any freedoms. They said that the people had little choice or decision-making power.

Mao was angry. He said that he had asked for one hundred flowers but had gotten weeds instead. He was bitter about the way intellectuals were criticizing him. Many of those intellectuals were rounded up by the government and sent away to labor camps—some for as long as 20 years!

The Great Leap Forward

After the "hundred flowers" campaign, Mao was stricter than ever. He clamped down on individual rights and liberties even more.

Mao knew that throughout history China's kings had tried to keep their country cut off from the rest of the world. But the rest of the world had been growing and expanding. It was time, as Mao put it, to "get China to walk on two feet." He intended to make China strong and powerful, so that it could grow as other nations had grown.

This project was called the Great Leap Forward. The idea was to turn one of China's problems—its huge population—into a plus. By using "people power," seven days a week, every day of the year, China would catch up with the rest of civilization.

As it turned out, the leap forward turned out to be several giant steps backward. Although the plan might have looked good on paper, it did not work well in practice.

Mao's officials organized people into large teams. These teams, known as cadres, ran factories, construction crews, and even farms. Historians tell us that some of these farming cadres were made up of more than one thousand people! The idea was that no one need ever be idle. Work could continue without interruption.

The biggest problem with the plan was that people in the cadres often did not know how to do their jobs. People who had never been on a farm were asked to plant and harvest. People who had never built a house were asked to saw and measure. Some learned quickly. Others were bored and did not care about their work. Soviet advisers who had come to China shook their heads in dismay. This plan, they thought, was all wrong. But Mao refused to listen.

The plan also called for moving industrial production out of the cities. There were millions of peasants who could make steel in the rural areas. Indeed, during the Great Leap Forward, peasants did try to make steel in backyard furnaces! They had no real idea how to do it, however. Many threw scrap metal, pots, and pans into the furnaces. The steel was usually of such poor quality that it could not be used.

The farming system was a failure, too. Two years of drought made a bad situation worse. Because of the lack of rain and the "who cares?" attitude of many of the farming cadres, crops were not planted correctly. As a result, there were no crops to harvest. More than 20 million people in China starved to death during the Great Leap Forward.

The Cultural Revolution

Mao did make some positive changes. He did away with the landlords who had cheated the peasants. However, by 1966, he had another kind of problem. Instead of a class of wealthy landlords, China now had classes of intellectuals, government workers, and business managers. They were controlling much of what went on.

Mao worried that China would turn away from the communist idea of a classless society. He called on the young people, particularly students. He urged them to seek out those who disagreed with his ideas and to get rid of them.

What happened over the next several years, which came to be called the Cultural Revolution, was a nightmare. A large number of students organized themselves into what was called the Red Guard. They did exactly as Mao had asked.

Their enemies were teachers, intellectuals, and others who had ever criticized Mao. Some people were simply humiliated in public—made to march through the streets wearing dunce caps. But many were tortured or killed. Others were sent to labor camps and forced to wash toilets or do other menial tasks. Many of these people were ridiculed and harassed so much that they committed suicide.

In addition to people, the Cultural Revolution looked for other enemies. Records, books, and paintings—anything that did not praise Mao or communism—were destroyed. The only book that was worshiped was the little red book of Mao's quotations. It was carried everywhere by the Red Guard.

Under Mao, China's many farms were taken away from rich land-lords and divided among the peasants, who were expected to grow crops for the country.

For several years, many schools and universities in China were closed. Teachers were either killed or sent away. More than 100 million Chinese children never learned to read or write because of the school closings.

Children were encouraged to turn in their parents if they were critical of Mao. Families were split up. Distrust and suspicion tore the country apart until Mao ended the Cultural Revolution in 1969. Mao spent the rest of his rule, until his death in 1976, trying to undo the damage his Cultural Revolution had caused.

THE CHINA OF DENG XIAOPING

The current leader of China is Deng Xiaoping. He is not the premier or the head of China's Communist party. These are titles that you might expect such a powerful man to hold. However, Deng prefers the title of vice chairman of the party. He has put his supporters in the important-sounding jobs. But he is still the most powerful figure in China today, even though he has turned over some of his power to Jiang Zemin.

Deng is a short man, with a face some have described as childlike. He wears the traditional buttoned jacket that most Chinese leaders wear. He wears socks of bright white—an unusual color in China. At 85, Deng looks gentle, smiling, and easygoing. His appearance is misleading, however, for he is known to be a man with an iron will.

Changes Had to Be Made

When Deng came to power in 1977, he knew China had to change. Although the country had accomplished some good things under Mao, its leader had made many mistakes.

China was too isolated from the rest of the world. Partly because of this isolation, and partly because of the Cultural Revolution, China's economy was in ruins. It was time to catch up. And to catch up, China would need to learn from other nations. "No more shutting the door on the world," Deng told his people.

Under Deng's leadership, China started a program called the Four Modernizations. Deng believed that four main areas needed improvement: military strength, science and technology, agriculture, and industry.

During the Cultural Revolution, many of China's brightest teachers and thinkers had been driven away by the Red Guard. Deng recalled some of these people. They were persuaded to come back to the universities and train a new generation of thinkers.

Deng also encouraged many of China's brightest students to study in foreign countries. He enthusiastically supported student-exchange programs. Under these programs, Chinese students attend school in Japan, Western Europe, and the United States.

The most powerful official in China today is Deng Xiaoping, the 85-year-old leader who rules China with an iron fist.

Changing Farms and Factories

Under communism, people are supposed to work for the good of all. A farmer in a communist country, for instance, must grow crops to feed people, not to make money. There were no incentives, no bonuses for growing more corn or taller grain. Under Mao Tse-tung, farms were changed to collective farms, with many people working as laborers.

The workers on collective farms did not work as hard as they did when they owned the land. They found it difficult to be interested in their jobs. Since they received the same salary whether they worked hard or not, many were not motivated to do their jobs well. Also, they did not seem to care about working for the good of the people.

Deng recognized that and changed the farming system. He broke up the huge collective farms and divided them into smaller plots of land. In addition, farmers are now allowed to make their own decisions about their work. If they want to grow potatoes, they grow potatoes. If they would rather grow beans, they do that. They may buy tractors or other equipment without permission from the government.

Some of the food that the farmers grow becomes the property of the government—China still has a communist economy. However, a portion of the farmers' crop now belongs to them. If they choose to sell their produce at neighborhood markets or roadside stands, they may. They set their own prices as well.

Factories also have been allowed more freedom. Deng has allowed individual factories to set their own prices. They make decisions, too, just as farmers do. Factory workers set production goals. Those who meet their goals are rewarded. They are given bonuses or higher wages.

Opening China to the World

Deng's changes have made China more open to the world. In 1984 President Reagan visited. In 1986 Queen Elizabeth of England made an official call.

As China's economy opened up, companies from foreign countries became interested in doing business there. Some branch offices of large corporations were established in the large cities of China. Now many American, Japanese, and European products are available in China. Billboards advertising Coca-Cola or Japanese cameras are a common sight.

With the increase in trade with people from other countries, there is a growing need for hotels and restaurants and for staffs of people to keep these businesses running. Furthermore, for the first time in its long history, China has become a tourist attraction. People are coming from all over the globe to see this newly opened country.

A Change in China's People

Deng has told his people that it is a glorious thing to be rich. He wants them to strive for wealth, for that will make the whole country wealthy. This is a complete reversal from Mao's thinking.

So far, China's people have embraced Deng's economic ideas. They, too, think it will be glorious to have more than the bare necessities. While most of their parents were lucky to own a radio, many Chinese today own tape decks, color televisions, and refrigerators.

In the years since Deng came to power, the average worker's income has doubled. People are becoming used to having and spending money. Young people are enjoying buying goods from the United States or Europe. Rock albums, blue jeans, and other items are in demand among Chinese teenagers.

China has made a great deal of progress during the rule of Deng Xiaoping. However, there have been serious problems. In fact, many people say the tragedy at Tiananmen Square happened as a result of these problems.

Before the Tiananmen Square massacre, tourism had become a major industry in China. Many people visited historic sites such as the Great Wall.

WHAT HAS GONE WRONG?

Under Deng's leadership, China's economy grew. What is more, people gained greater control over their own incomes. However, the Chinese people still did not have a say in the politics of their country.

The Communist party, the powerful force behind the government, remained strongly in control. Other than making money, people still had little personal freedom. The government told people where they should live. It controlled the policies in every neighborhood and district. People had no say whatsoever in who represented them. The government even dictated that families could have only one child, to keep population growth to a minimum.

This kind of closed government was a disappointment to many Chinese. Some had been to school overseas and had seen firsthand what democracy was like. They liked the idea of having freedom of speech. They liked the idea of being able to question the government leaders. The open, free exchange of ideas these students had learned about was not allowed in China.

Corruption: An "Everyday Nuisance"

Students and many other citizens also were concerned about the growing corruption in their country. Corruption is any dishonesty, but most especially among government officials. Many

28

China has begun to develop economic ties with other countries.
Western products like Pepsi are often enjoyed by the Chinese
people.

people thought that although the government was a strong force, it was not doing one of its jobs—watching out for corruption. Several times during the spring of 1989, journalists had discovered government workers doing illegal things. However, the government stopped the journalists from printing their findings.

Most people in China have always been aware of the dishonesty of government workers, anyway. It is, as one Chinese woman puts it, "an everyday nuisance, in every city and town in China."

Part of the reason for this dishonesty is that the government is slow moving. It takes months and months to make simple decisions. Often people find that they can get results more quickly by dealing directly with an official. By offering the official a large sum of money—a bribe—the decision can be made on the spot!

Many Chinese people complain that *who* one knows is more important than *what* one knows. A pregnant woman planning for the birth of her baby, for example, might want to deliver it in a particular hospital. Maybe the nurses there are especially good, or maybe the hospital has a good reputation for dealing with problem births. If that woman wants to guarantee that she will be able to deliver her child in that particular hospital, she needs to know "the right people." It may involve a bribe of money or a favor.

The same applies in other areas. If a man wants to get a small loan to start up a business, he has to find an official who can be bribed somehow. Parents who want to get their children into the best kindergartens often resort to bribery, too. By simply "letting the request go through proper channels," the slow workings of government (called bureaucracy) will most likely not get the job done.

There is a Chinese word for such everyday bribery—it is called *quanxi*. *Quanxi* is so common that most people don't make much of an issue of it. One fairly wealthy Chinese woman with a family estimated that she and her friends spend three out of every four hours a day using *quanxi*!

The Beginnings of Student Unrest

By 1989 the corruption, as well as the Communist government's tight control of their lives, had angered many students. Also upsetting was the rising cost of many items. Inflation was becoming a bigger and bigger problem.

However, what sent the young people of China into Tiananmen Square for the first time was the death of a man named Hu Yaobang. Once a powerful government figure, he had become a hero to many students. He had stood up for some students who were protesting back in 1986. Because he had sided with the students, Hu had been fired from his post. On April 15, 1989, he had suffered a heart attack and died.

Thousands of students marched into Tiananmen Square after hearing the news of Hu's death. They carried signs that read: "Hu, you are precious in death." Many of the students felt that this would be a good time to show their feelings about Deng and his government, too. Those signs were not as gracious. Some of them called for Deng to step down from his powerful position. Others

The demonstration in Tiananmen Square was begun by students mourning the death of Hu Yaobang, a government official fired from his post for supporting student protests.

were less severe. They called for Deng and other officials to allow free speech and expression. They called for an end to the tight control of Chinese communism.

"The Students Are Very Pure"

More than 10,000 students from Beijing University began their march to the square. It was a distance of ten miles. Along the way, other students joined them.

They tried to keep their march orderly. Witnesses to the first days of the march say that the students were charming and polite. They thanked police, who were standing by in case there was any trouble. "We appreciate you, people's police!" they chanted.

As the students made their way through the square, many bystanders cheered their support. Children and their mothers waved to them. One elderly man exclaimed, "The students are very pure!" Another onlooker said, "I want the same things the students want. I want my child to have those things."

Workers wearing yellow hard hats waved and cheered. They also signaled their approval another way: They banged chopsticks against their tin lunch pails! Other workers threw food and cigarettes to the students from windows and rooftops.

Hunger Strikers

At least one thousand students decided to go on hunger strikes when they got to the square. A hunger strike is a person's decision to stop eating until his or her demands are met. In many instances, a hunger striker prefers to starve to death rather than to back down.

In this case, the students wanted to call attention to their demands for changes in government policy. They wanted to show that they were willing to die for their cause. The hunger strikers sat on the pavement in the square. As they became weaker and weaker, their friends fixed up mats for them to lie on. When it rained, sheets of plastic were strung up. The mats were placed underneath to stay dry. Over the next several weeks, two thousand more students decided to strike in this way.

Upstaging a Visitor

By the beginning of May, there still had not been any violence. Police continued to keep track of the crowd. However, the police were greatly outnumbered. More people were joining the demonstrators each day. The number of nonstudents was growing. Coal miners, farmers, elderly people, railroad workers—all took their places in Tiananmen Square.

Deng and his government officials were very concerned. They knew that the hunger strikers and the demonstrators were getting a lot of attention. Newspapers from all over the world were reporting the massive demonstrations. It looked as if Deng had lost control of his country.

Soviet leader Mikhail Gorbachev met with Deng Xiaoping while the student protests were going on in Tiananmen Square. It was the first time the leaders of the world's two largest Communist countries had met in 30 years—and they were upstaged by the students!

The upcoming visit of Soviet leader Mikhail Gorbachev was a problem, too. Since the days of Mao Tse-tung, the Chinese and the Soviets had been enemies. Each nation had its own brand of communism. The two nations had a common border, and each was suspicious that the other would try to invade it. Their mutual dislike was known around the world.

But Gorbachev was interested in healing old wounds. He wanted to visit China and to talk with Deng. The arrival of Gorbachev would be the first time a Soviet leader had met with a Chinese leader in 30 years! The visit was scheduled for May 15. With the huge demonstration going on in the square, what would happen?

The visit was a disaster. Although the two leaders met and posed for cameras, there was a lot of tension. An elaborate welcoming ceremony was supposed to have been held in Tiananmen Square. Instead, a smaller ceremony was held at the airport.

Gorbachev was supposed to have laid a wreath in the square. He clearly could not do that, either. The stars of the visit were not Deng and Gorbachev. The spotlight was on the growing crowds (close to one million) in Tiananmen Square. Deng was angry and embarrassed.

On May 20 he put the country under martial law. That meant that soldiers were being called in to restore order. Deng told his advisers that his army of three million could handle the trouble.

News spread quickly through the crowds of demonstrators. Although few thought Deng would order an outright attack, just to be on the safe side, a warning was sounded. People who had heard about the soldiers banged pots and pans. The noise was to alert the students that there could be trouble.

The Goddess
of Democracy

Meanwhile, to insult Deng further, the students in the square built a statue. It was in the shape of a woman holding a torch. Everyone could see that the 27-foot-tall statue looked like the Statue of Liberty. The students called their creation the Goddess of Democracy. It was a symbol of the freedom and democracy they wanted. Perhaps it was also meaningful that the statue was not built to last forever. It was made of Styrofoam and plaster of Paris.

More than 250,000 people filed before the Goddess of Democracy. Many of them wept, calling the idea "beautiful." However, the government had an announcement blaring from a loudspeaker. The recorded message shouted: "This statue is illegal. It has not been approved by the government."

The Army Arrives

The coming of the army turned out not to be a danger at first. The first troops were young and carried no weapons. Perhaps the government thought that just their presence would frighten the students. It did not.

The young soldiers, members of the 38th Division, were met by demonstrators before they got into the square. Some students threw garbage, while others begged the soldiers to stop their march. The army did stop. In fact, many of the young soldiers were in agreement with the students. Some of them stripped off their uniform shirts and threw them aside. They took their places with the cheering students.

However, older, more experienced troops were brought in later. These soldiers, the 27th Division, had orders to destroy the demonstration. They ordered the 38th Division to fire on the crowd. When the young soldiers of the 38th refused, the 27th Division opened fire on those soldiers themselves!

The 38th then began to attack the students. They smashed the Goddess of Democracy and began the slaughter that shocked the world.

AFTER TIANANMEN SQUARE

In the weeks after the massacre at Tiananmen Square, China tried to get back to normal. The government denied that the army attack had taken place. Instead, it blamed the incident on a "handful of rioters with guns." Deng even went so far as to accuse other nations of supplying the "hooligans" with their weapons.

To symbolize their desire for freedom, the students in Tiananmen Square built the Goddess of Democracy, which closely resembled the Statue of Liberty.

"Thank You for Your Hard Work"

As for the army's action, it was sheer bravery, according to Deng's government. Government officials claimed that the army had tried to keep from firing back at the crowd. They said that the "hooligans and rioters" were so violent that the soldiers had had to respond with their weapons. The government still does not want to admit it issued attack orders. It does not want the world to know that it ordered soldiers to kill thousands of unarmed Chinese students.

Instead, the soldiers were congratulated on national television by the government. "Thank you for your hard work," said a top government official, Li Peng. "You must be exhausted."

"It's Like the Cultural Revolution All Over Again"

While they treated the soldiers like heroes, the government arrested many student leaders. One news article reported that more than two hundred student leaders were jailed in Qincheng Prison near Beijing. They were charged with taking part in activities "against the Communist government." Some—no one knows how many—were executed for their parts in the demonstration.

Deng and his government know that many other student leaders have not yet been caught. The government has been trying to arrest those who organized the demonstration. It also has encouraged people to "watch and listen." Anyone who hears of a student leader is encouraged to turn in that student's name to the police. Any citizen who knows of a leader and fails to turn him or her in can be arrested. So many Chinese are living in fear.

Hundreds have been arrested in this way. One student leader was turned in by his sister. The government's practice of encouraging people to spy on one another makes many Chinese angry. One man muttered, "It's like the Cultural Revolution all over again!"

Such reporting can backfire, however, and in some cases it already has. Some people who have been turned in are totally innocent. Those who reported them may have had grudges against them or grievances that had nothing to do with the student demonstrations. There was even a case of workers turning in their bosses because the bosses had denied them raises!

Reaction from Around the World

The attack at Tiananmen Square shocked people around the world. Leaders from the United States and Europe sharply criticized Deng and his government.

In the United States, many people wanted President Bush to impose economic sanctions on China. Sanctions are bans on trade with another country. A country may impose sanctions on another to show its displeasure. China depends on world trade to keep its economy balanced. If nations refuse to trade with China, it will be without those goods it cannot produce itself.

President Bush imposed some sanctions immediately after the massacre. He urged the World Bank to suspend a $1 billion loan to China. He also stopped a shipment of military equipment that was on its way to China. (The United States has been helping China modernize its F-8 bomber.)

Some Americans think more restrictions and sanctions should be imposed. They think the United States should cut off all ties with China. Others think the United States should keep channels open. They argue that China is an important ally to have and to refuse to trade with China would be foolish. Permanent bad feelings might then exist between the two nations, and these people worry that such a split might someday hurt the United States.

A Great Leap Backward

No matter what sanctions the United States imposes, China's economy has been hurt by the massacre. Many large corporations have branch offices in China. They employ many people and put millions of dollars into the economy.

After the massacre, however, most of these companies left. Some closed their doors only temporarily, but others have no

During the Tiananmen Square uprising, people around the world showed their support for the students by holding demonstrations like this one at the Chinese embassy in Washington, D.C.

intention of going back. Some business experts have called Deng's actions a "great leap backward."

"Only a few days ago, we thought everything looked fine," said an employee of Owens-Corning Fiberglass, an American firm located in Beijing. "Then, wham! You have to wonder about the stability of the whole regime."

An executive of a European import company agreed. "What China promised to investors was stability. Stupidly, we believed them."

An Uncertain Future

No one knows what the future will be for China and its people. Although Deng and the government insist that the massacre never took place, the people talk of little else. Almost everyone in Beijing has a family member or friend who was killed or injured in the attack.

"Of course, we will never forget," said one young woman. "Democracy is in the people's hearts now—it can never be erased."

FACTS ABOUT CHINA

Capital: Beijing

Population: 1.1 billion

Form of government: Communist dictatorship

Official language: Chinese

Chief products:

> Agriculture: rice, wheat, cotton, tea, soybeans
> Manufacturing: iron, steel, machinery, textiles

Glossary

bribe *An illegal offer of money in exchange for a favor.*

bureaucracy *A government run by many different departments. There is always much "red tape," or excessive detail, in a bureaucracy.*

cadres *Large teams of workers.*

communism *A system in which there is no private property. All businesses, goods, and land are owned in common.*

corruption *Bribery or other dishonesty among government officials.*

hunger strike *A protest in which a person refuses to eat.*

inflation *Rising costs of goods.*

intellectual *A scholar or well-informed person.*

martial law *A system imposed by a government when there is a war or other emergency. Under martial law, soldiers perform many of the duties of ordinary police. Strict rules are usually enforced during this time.*

massacre *The cruel killing of a large number of helpless or unresisting people.*

peasant *A poor farmer.*

quanxi *A Chinese word describing the common, everyday corruption that is practiced throughout China.*

sanctions *Strict bans on trade used by one nation against another. Sanctions are used against a nation to express displeasure with its policies.*

Index